ALASKA REFLECTIONS

Alaska Reflections

Reflections of the Wilderness Series

by

LARRY RICE

Photographs by Larry Rice

ICS BOOKS, INC.
Merrillville, Indiana

Alaska Reflections

Dedication

This book is dedicated to Judy Bradford, my wife, trip companion, best friend, and ruthless live-in editor. Facing off a grizzly bear was so much more fun with her at my side.

Published by:
ICS Books, Inc.
1370 E. 86th Place
Merrillville, IN 46410
800-541-7323

Co-Published in Canada by:
Vanwell Publishing LTD.
1 Northrup Crescent, P.O. Box 2131,
St. Catharines, Ontario L2M 6P5
800-661-6136

Library of Congress Cataloging-in-Publication Data

Rice, Larry, 1950–
    Alaska reflections / written by Larry Rice ; photographs by Larry Rice.
        p. cm. — (Reflections of the wilderness)
    Includes index.
    ISBN 0-934802-04-1 : $11.99
1. Alaska—Description and travel. 2. Alaska—Pictorial works. 3. Natural his-
    tory—Alaska. 4. Natural history—Alaska—Pictorial works. I. Title. II. Series.
    F910.5.R527 1993
    917.98—dc20   93-11578
                                              CIP

Table of Contents

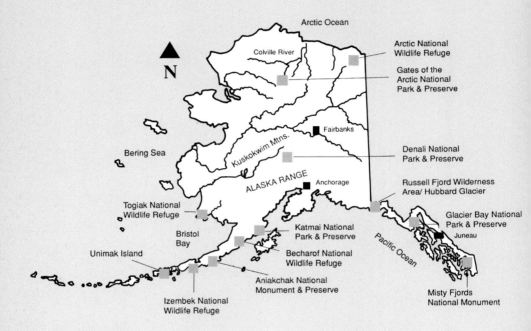

Arctic Ocean

Colville River

Arctic National
Wildlife Refuge

Gates of the
Arctic National
Park & Preserve

N

Fairbanks

Bering Sea

Kuskokwim Mtns.

ALASKA RANGE

Denali National
Park & Preserve

Anchorage

Russell Fjord Wilderness
Area/ Hubbard Glacier

Togiak National
Wildlife Refuge

Glacier Bay National
Park & Preserve

Bristol
Bay

Katmai National
Park & Preserve

Juneau

Unimak Island

Becharof National
Wildlife Refuge

Pacific Ocean

Izembek National
Wildlife Refuge

Aniakchak National
Monument & Preserve

Misty Fjords
National Monument

The Great Land

Alaska! To the Aleuts who have lived here for thousands of years it is "the Great Land." Today, our forty-ninth state represents the last remaining true wilderness in the United States. Aldo Leopold, whose book *A Sand County Almanac* became the bible of the environmental movement of the 1960s and early 1970s, wrote that wilderness encompasses many things, but more than anything else it is a place "big enough to absorb a two-weeks' pack trip, and kept devoid of roads, artificial trails, cottages, or other works of man." In Alaska there are still many places large enough to absorb backcountry trips of a month or more without encountering artifacts of today's civilized society.

Alaska is a land of extremes: from untracked wilderness to fast track cities; windswept arctic deserts to lush rain forests; tidewater glaciers to muskeg bogs; one-ounce shrews to half-ton bears. John Muir, the outspoken turn-of-the-century conservationist, declared that "no other part of the Earth known to man surpasses Alaska in imposing and beautiful scenery." His words still ring true today. Alaska is a place so immense that its size is difficult to comprehend. First-time visitors are usually overwhelmed. Even most residents know little about this big country in which they reside.

Consider:

Alaska ranges across four time zones and encompasses an area about 2.2 times the size of the state of Texas. It occupies both the Western and the Eastern hemispheres.

Alaska has 50 percent more coastline than *all* the lower forty-eight states combined and is washed by two major oceans and three major seas.

Alaska has more than 365,000 miles of rivers, and ten rivers are longer than 300 miles. There are three *million* lakes; eighteen hundred named islands, rocks, and reefs; nineteen mountains higher than fourteen thousand feet; and more than half of the earth's glaciers.

Alaska has fewer people than the city of San Francisco. About 75 percent of the residents live in urban areas, leaving over 95 percent of the state uninhabited.

Alaska's total protected acreage—national parks, national forests, wild and scenic rivers, and national wildlife refuges—make up an area larger than the combined states of California, Indiana, and Pennsylvania.

Alaska's statistics are impressive, but by themselves they are nothing but trivia; when combined with the physical experience of Alaska, the facts and individual characteristics are somehow no longer measurable or describable, and that is the magic that makes backcountry Alaska special. It is a place that is accessible, but not easy, for those who want the experience of self-sufficiency in a remote and untamed environment. Wilderness is more than a physical place, however. It is an idea. As Wallace Stegner observed, wilderness is sanity in an insane world and the backdrop against which our national character was formed. Its continued existence is reassuring and "good for our spiritual health even if we never once in ten years set foot in it."

For anyone who does visit, be forewarned. Henry Gannett, the renowned cartographer of the American West, offered this advice in 1899 to anyone contemplating a trip to Alaska: "If you are old go by all means; but if you are young stay away until you grow older. The scenery of Alaska is so much grander than anything else of the kind in the world that, once beheld, all other scenery becomes flat and insipid. It is not well to dull one's capacity for such enjoyment by seeing the finest first."

Contrary to what ol' Henry said, I found that after trips to Alaska my appreciation for our little pockets of preservation here in the lower forty-eight was increased. I could better imagine the grandeur and rugged beauty that have been lost, and feel a greater resolve and urgency to protect what we have remaining.

FOUR ALASKAS TO VISIT

Each region of the state is distinctive not only in terms of geography and climate but also in regard to what type of activity it provides. For this book I have selected photos and reflections that I hope will both express the essence of Alaska's pristine landscape and wildlife and communicate my own experiences of joy and frustration, fright and exhilaration—the whole myriad of human response to the wilderness revealed.

CHAPTER 1

The Southeast

Nicknamed the Panhandle, this 560-mile-long, 30-mile-wide strip of land stretching along Canada's western border is rated by many as the most scenic region in Alaska. Spruce-covered mountains—the highest coastal range in the world—rise abruptly from the seashore. Glaciers spill over into mountain valleys, which are often penetrated by deep salt-water fjords. Evergreen rain forests—lush with ferns, mosses, hemlock, and cedar—are home to grizzly and black bears, black-tailed deer, wolves, moose, and bald eagles. And along the coast are thousands of islands that create protected inland passages where whales, porpoises, and seals cavort.

MISTY FJORDS NATIONAL MONUMENT

The Misty Fjords National Monument is a 2.3-million-acre unit within the Tongass National Forest. As the name implies, the area is continually shrouded in a heavy, damp mist. As our Cessna 185 floatplane flew over the thick, dark forest and high cliffs a thousand feet below, a steady wind whipped up waves on the water and a light rain fell. Our home in Illinois seemed another world away.

Kayaking is not always a wild white water experience. Choked with grasses, parts of the fjord are very slow going indeed. We were not in a hurry, however. Much more interested in what Thoreau called "the tonic of wilderness," we drank deeply and gave ourselves over to the experience.

The forest does not care if you have nowhere to put your tent. We finally put ours on a tiny, lumpy patch just above the high tide line. Rising twenty stories above us, massive specimens of Sitka spruce, cedar, and hemlock blocked out all but the most persistent rays of sunlight, while at our feet delicate ferns and wild orchids decorated the twisted, rotting skeletons of the fallen giants.

In this land of superlatives the bugs are not an aberration. They are big, and there are a lot of them. A steady breeze is enough to deter them, but once the breeze drops, the swarms of hungry, buzzing, biting mosquitoes and flies become blinding. The mosquitoes are rather bumbling and easy to kill, but the whitesox (a white-legged blackfly) are almost unbearable. Their bite is painless, but an hour later the area itches maddeningly and oozes blood. Insect repellent is useless against these super-bugs (they laugh in the face of DEET); one's only recourse is to wear a heavy-duty head net, or better yet, zip oneself in one's tent.

(*Above*) It may be hard to imagine ever being hot in Alaska, but there are times when one might actually be so moved as to complain about the heat. And what better way to cool off than going for a dip in the cold waters of an Alaskan fjord. Judy went first, boldly wading over the slippery intertidal rocks covered by an assortment of seaweed, starfish, barnacles, clams, and urchins. Finally reaching deeper water, she plunged into the ocean only to shoot right back out screaming in ecstasy and pain. Meanwhile, I stood at the water's edge, buck-naked except for my rubber knee-high boots. "Come on in," Judy cajoled while doing a backstroke. "It feels great!" I did, but I am here to tell you that swimming in an Alaskan fjord will never be a popular recreational sport.

(*Left, facing page*) The black bear is the most common bear in North America. Adults range from 5 to 6 feet long and can weigh anywhere between 200 and 600 pounds. This particular bear seemed harmless, almost clownish, as he munched on his snack of lush beach grass, clods of dirt and all. *Ursus americanus* is not to be laughed at, however. The black bear has killed more humans than the dreaded grizzly. We backed slowly toward the kayak, careful not to trip or make jerky movements. The bear eventually grew tired of eating and ambled off up a brush-choked creek. Not wanting to be fooled by a bear, we waited a few more minutes and then hurried to the kayak and headed back to camp.

As you might expect, Glacier Bay is full of glaciers. Kayaking along the edge of any of them you can easily find an inviting crack to explore. This particular crack opened into a shallow cave, dimly lit by filtered sunlight. The enormous pressure created by the weight of the glacier squeezes the air out of the ice, turning it from the regular pale white to shades of luminous blue. Huge rocks and smatterings of gravel hung suspended in the clear, hard coldness, trapped for perhaps hundreds of years in the belly of this slowly lumbering leviathan.

(Above) Fjords are very narrow inlets of the sea, huge submerged valleys that were carved from the earth by long since melted glaciers. Often they are several thousand feet deep, even at the shore where the sheer cliffs rise hundreds of feet up. Paddling in these narrow channels can be humbling as the creaking, cracking, crashing sounds of ice and rock falls echo in low rumbles off the cliffs. Here on the icebergs as many as twenty-five hundred harbor seals spend their summer vacation, like so many tourists crammed on a sunny beach. Safe from their chief enemy, the killer whale, they mate and raise their pups.

(Right, facing page) This one-room cabin was built in Reid Inlet by Joe Ibach in 1940. He and his wife, Muz, hauled bag after bag of dirt from their homestead on an island in Icy Strait to build a terraced vegetable garden. The spruce seedlings that Muz planted back then are now over twenty-five feet high, the only ones of their size this far north in the bay. Joe was a prospector and had originally come to Glacier Bay in 1929. Although he had objected to its becoming a national monument, he stayed in the area (which eventually grew to contain 4,135,269 acres) for over thirty years, during which time he and his wife became part of Glacier Bay's lore and history. Muz died in 1959, and in the spring of 1960 Joe visited the cabin one last time. The twenty-year-old tiny cabin—with only a bed, table and chairs, and stove for furnishings, and decorated with "wallpaper" from pages torn out of catalogs—must have seemed like an old friend to him that last day as he reflected on the hard and beautiful wilderness life he and his wife had shared here. He sat down at his rickety table and wrote a will, ending with the words, "There's a time to live and a time to die. This is the time." And then Joe Ibach shot himself.

(*Above*) Pushed on by their own weight, glaciers flow like rivers, the ice in the middle moving quicker than that on the sides. The path of Johns Hopkins Glacier was unmistakable as we watched it "flow" into the sea. Seeing a glacier like this, a force that moves maybe a couple centimeters a day, instills a great respect for these natural bulldozers that have taken thousands of years to carve out valleys in the earth that are bigger than some states. Upon his first view of the Glacier Bay area, John Muir thought it "a solitude of ice and snow and newborn rocks, dim, dreary, mysterious." And so it is.

(*Left, facing page*) There's a strange persistence you have when you're hiking up a mountain. At first you notice everything, looking around you with wide eyes trying to take it all in. Every bush, twig, and flower is more beautiful than the one before, and every bird or wriggling little creature deserves a photograph. After you've been at it a couple hours, however, steadily climbing, your feet go slower and your eyes look more toward the ground in front of you, the cry of a bird now hardly worth the energy to glance upward. The view at your feet is sparse; low arctic willows and dryas, bits of moss and tiny herbs; and finally, nothing but loose, unstable boulders slick with verglas. Once at the top, however, everything is amazing again as you gaze tiredly around full circle, trying to draw energy from the height and view. At thirty-five hundred feet we encountered a flock of gray-crowned rosy finches, who arrived out of nowhere to drink at the pool at our feet. The tame little birds then hopped comically to a nearby snowbank where they feasted on iceworms, needle-sized black worms that feed on the algae growing in the snow. Once sated, the finches lifted off, disappearing in a whir of wings.

Suddenly we felt very alone as we watched the Cessna lift slowly off the water. We knew the pilot was heading back to his family in Yakutat, probably soon to watch the evening news or "Wheel of Fortune" on television. It seemed ironic here on this lonely beach at the head of Russell Fjord, watching the small plane drone off in the distance, that only yesterday we had been caught up in the frenetic rush of the world's busiest airport, O'Hare International in Chicago, where dozens of superjets take off every hour. The silence became deafening.

Glaciers have a way of sneaking up on you sometimes. Some formerly slothful glaciers, particularly in the Commonwealth of Independent States, Iceland, and Alaska, suddenly seem to wake up and begin moving at a rapid pace, up to five meters an hour. These "galloping" glaciers eventually calm down again after a year or two. Within a few months, this quiet area of Russell Fjord became Russell Lake, its water level eighty feet higher than sea level. Later that year the ice dam broke and the area returned to normal.

Kayaking is not recommended in conditions such as this. Giant ice cube boulders shed from Hubbard Glacier during the night choked the fjord until mid-morning when they drifted away with the flood tide.

CHAPTER 2

The Southwest

Worldworld-famous for its sportfishing lakes and streams and giant brown bears, southwest Alaska consists of the Alaska Peninsula, which extends for 550 miles into the Pacific Ocean; the Aleutian Islands, which continue for another 1,500 miles toward Asia; and the coastal area south of the Norton Sound. This is the area affected by two of the world's most tempestuous bodies of water, the North Pacific and the stormy Bering Sea. The volcanoes and sloping grasslands of the Alaska Peninsula are connected to the rest of western Alaska by the lowlands and marshes surrounding Bristol Bay. In the Aleutians, noted biologist Olaus Murie observed that "arctic and alpine merge." Animal life converges here from all directions and from both Asia and North America.

KATMAI NATIONAL PARK AND PRESERVE

At the northern end of the Alaska Peninsula is the four-million-acre Katmai National Park and Preserve, home to the largest population of unhunted brown bears in the world. Grizzlies love to play in the water, cooling off their huge furry bodies in the icy lake. They are both great swimmers and great fishermen, feasting off the abundant salmon they grab effortlessly from the shallows.

Feeling like modern-day *voyageurs,* for three days we explored the maze of coves and inlets that make up the Bay of Islands. Birds were abundant: bald eagles, gulls, grebes, ducks, swans, and the ever-present loon, whose laughing cry seemed to mock us as we paddled. At one point a pair of river otters apparently decided we were enough of a novelty to warrant further attention. They interrupted their own play to chase us, diving and resurfacing around our boat all afternoon. Having finally had their fill of our uninterrupted paddling, they eventually left us. Tired from our day's efforts, at night we camped on rocky shores, lulled to sleep by the cacophony of animal and insect noises.

(*Above*) Cats are cats everywhere. This Canada lynx was no exception. Having disrupted our dinner with its maniacal cry (we were certain there was a lunatic roaming the woods—a thought more troubling than the possibility of encountering a grizzly), the disdainful feline stepped daintily over the pumice and gravel, hardly bothering to glance at us as we stood watching it twenty yards away. It spent some time licking its paw, glanced at us again, then melted off into the alders.

(*Left, facing page*) This gently rolling scene with its close-cropped mat of plants and moss is deceptive: it took us hours of struggling through deep, scratching grass, mucky bogs, and shoulder-high brush before we reached this serene alpine tundra. The area's inhabitants include ptarmigan, hoary marmots, and ground squirrels, all of which are food for the golden eagles and grizzlies that also live here. In the distance is a string of lakes which we still had to paddle.

BECHAROF NATIONAL WILDLIFE REFUGE

The North American brown bear, the Alaskan brown bear, the grizzly, the Kodiak, *Ursus arctos*—whatever the name, this bear once ranged over western North America from Mexico to Alaska. Practically extinct in the lower 48 states, over most of Alaska these bears are faring quite well. On this particular trip my friend Clyde and I were kayaking in the Becharof National Wildlife Refuge, a 1.2-million-acre preserve with lakes, volcanic peaks, wetlands, and tundra-covered hills. We came upon the bears apparently in the middle of a nice salmon feast; they were all busy at the water's edge obviously trying to catch a fish. Salmon carcasses littered the beach. They must have been at it for some time. Suddenly the furry fishermen lifted their snouts and sniffed the wind. Quickly they shuffled away as one of the biggest bears I have ever seen blustered over the ridge and down the bank. It soon became apparent that this was *his* beach and we were not welcome. He reared up and manwalked to the edge of the lake. He growled low in his throat. He dropped back to the earth with a force that seemed to send shock waves that pushed our boat backward. We felt lucky to be on the water (grizzlies can run up to 30 miles per hour on land). No idiots, we were just getting ready to leave when the bear began to wade into the water. When he was up to his neck, we realized he was preparing to swim after us! Having no idea how fast grizzlies can swim, we lost no time in getting out of there.

A trade-off for all the great views in Alaska is often lousy weather, which of course obscures the views. During the short hour at Becharof Lake when it was not rainy, windy, and cloudy, we could actually see Mount Peulik, five miles south.

Northwest of Mount Peulik and a mile south of Becharof Lake lie two volcanic craters called *maars*. Formed by an explosion caused by a build up of pressure within the earth, these craters are located in one of Alaska's most recently active volcanic sites and are known as the Ukinrek Maars. I could only guess how big these strange reservoirs are or what the water at their bottoms is like. I was content to take pictures a safe distance from the edge.

A caldera is a volcano whose top has collapsed, leaving a large bowl-shaped depression. The Aniakchak Caldera, one of the world's largest, occupies thirty square miles and is twenty-five hundred feet deep. The park itself covers 600,000 acres and is located in the middle of the Alaska Peninsula. Aniakchak last erupted in 1931, and the charred remains of some of that activity still linger.

(Above) "Caldera" is Spanish for caldron, an apt name when you look at the southern rim, where the clouds flow over the sides like steam in some magic witches brew: "Double double toil and trouble/ Fire burn and caldron bubble."

(Right and facing page) Despite the initial bleak appearance of the caldera landscape, Surprise Lake and the surrounding area were comparatively a riot of color. Bubbling springs on the caldera floor spit forth rusty water that flowed into the emerald lake. The springs were crowded with red algae, and pockets of ash around the mucky shoreline grew brave sedges, horsetails, grasses, marsh marigolds, and forbs.

29

Caribou are herd animals. This caribou and her calf thus appear to have gotten separated and inadvertently wandered into a wasteland, but they are actually taking a shortcut to better grazing grounds. They didn't notice us until we were very close. In chance encounters such as this it suddenly becomes a challenge to observe as long as possible without disturbing. You hold your breath. You stand still for amazingly long periods. And then they see you and gallop away. You release the tension of the last few minutes, relishing the rush of exhilaration that washes over.

One thing about exploring a volcanic area: when it is windy, there is dust everywhere. You eat dust. Here, the wind was so strong it threatened to blow us, tents and all, into Surprise Lake. The lake itself was rolling with whitecaps, and swirls of ash filled the air. "So foul and fair a day I have not seen."

The Aniakchak River empties out of Surprise Lake through a narrow defile called the Gates. The rapids were not dangerous, but they kept you on your toes. Twisting, bending, tossing, bouncing, I worked to pull the raft through the rollers while Mike kept us on course and away from boulders. Speeding by toward the Pacific Ocean, we could only just notice the landscape: low-rolling tundra hills; scrubby willows and alders along the high riverbank; caribou along the ridges; and an occasional red fox darting in and out of the foliage along the bank. Of course, there was griz sign everywhere. In a single day of rafting we counted twenty-two of the great bruins.

If you're a black brant (a small marine goose), Izembek National Wildlife Refuge, at the tip of the Alaska Peninsula, is the place to be in September. All 250,000 of them come here both for a change of scenery from their nesting grounds in northern Alaska, Canada, and Siberia and to eat eelgrass. (Eelgrass is an aquatic plant that looks and smells like coleslaw.) Needless to say, with a quarter-million geese honking and flapping all over the place, we did not get much sleep. At dawn their slumber-party prattle became a great honking din as scores of them raced off to the eelgrass beds or waddled out to the water.

Every now and then one chances upon an old trapper's cabin, a welcome change of pace from all the stooped tent camping. Happily, there were no bears inside; the only animal we supplanted was a long-tailed weasel. After we'd cleaned the place up a bit we were feeling right at home, with plenty of head and elbow room and a strong tin roof overhead to keep out the rain.

Most of Izembek Refuge looks like this: low-growing sub-arctic heath, wide open for miles around. Looking around full circle you can easily spot a roving bear or a bald eagle, and you realize that you are a very long way from anywhere and it's a long walk back.

With a brave smile in the ice-cold water we gingerly waded through the thigh-deep stream. Salmon were everywhere, the large silvery schools swimming out of our way like drilling cadets. Adult salmon mature in the ocean and then return to freshwater to spawn. During their journey they change from their usual silvery color to a variety of brighter shades, depending on the species. The males develop hooked jaws, and we could see several of these locked in combat with each other, their mouths clamped over each other's faces. During this time the salmon take no food, and by the time they arrive at the spawning beds, often having battled rapids and jumped up high falls, they are completely exhausted. They spawn and then die. Their carcasses become easy pickings for bears, eagles, and other fish-eaters.

"About 150 feet ahead were three grizzlies," wrote Bob Marshall, inveterate explorer of the Brooks Range. "This may seem like a long distance to a catcher trying to throw a man out stealing second, but not to a man faced by three bears, 11 miles from the closest gun, 106 from the first potential stretcher bearer, and 300 miles from the nearest hospital."

As the day wound down I sat half hidden on a knoll, the wide view before me. Watching the tranquil scene below, bathed in the dusty orange of dusk, I could think of no other place in the world more important to be.

UNIMAK ISLAND, ALASKA MARITIME NATIONAL WILDLIFE REFUGE

One tends to associate volcanoes with tropical climates, but Alaska has several active ones. "The sentinel of the North Pacific," Shishaldin Volcano (9,372 feet) is the highest peak in the Aleutians and has long been a landmark for passing mariners, that is when they could actually see it. The weather is normally wet, stormy, and foggy.

"Seems as if something unknown were possibly lurking in those bushes, or solitary places. Nay, it is quite certain there is—some vital unseen presence." Whatever Walt Whitman was writing about, this quote expressed our feeling of apprehension when in grizzly country. We walked cautiously, carefully scanning the area and quickly turning at the slightest noise.

There was no path, and once begun, we had to continue. Like the Prince on his way to Sleeping Beauty's castle, we battled the thick growth, twigs slapping our faces, rootwads snaring our feet. We were literally walking in the trees and had no idea which way we were going. Out. Our greatest fear was stumbling upon a sleeping brown bear.

The brilliant colors of the plant life are often in sharp contrast to the grey, stormy skies. Like a delectable cake, such rich scenery is hard to take in all at once, despite the desire to gobble it up whole.

The end of the line. The climb to the summit was made through a dense fog that only lifted at the last minute to reveal a wide chasm separating us from our goal. Clearly there was nowhere else to go but down.

The bald eagle is the only eagle solely native to North America. Once killed by the thousands in Alaska because of its interference with salmon fishing, the bird is now protected in all fifty states. This eagle's nest was a hundred feet below us, a large jumble of sticks more than two feet across built on a narrow shelf. The two nearly full-grown eaglets inside were carefully guarded by both parents, who soared close by, intimidating us with their cold, yellow stare.

CHAPTER 3

The Interior and The West

Variety and extremes are the passwords in this region, where the terrain varies from the continent's loftiest peak (Mount McKinley, 20,320 feet), to the low flats of the Yukon River and the shores of Bristol Bay. Here, the state's highest and lowest temperatures have been recorded, and wildlife ranges from grizzly, moose, and Dall sheep to walrus, sea lions, and seals. Millions of sea birds frequent the offshore waters of Cape Peirce and Cape Newenham, while in the interior thousands of sandhill cranes pass through in spring and fall migrations. Denali is Alaska's best-known park; in the height of summer you may have to wait a few days to obtain a backcountry permit. In most other areas away from the towns and villages, however, solitude is easy to find.

Alaska may seem like a long way to travel to go skiing, but once there, there is no comparison. We skied in the tundra between the Alaska Range to the south and a smaller range of mountains to the north. Completely exposed on the flat, desolate plain, we were constantly whipped by the fierce wind. Our only relief came when we encountered the small forests of windsheared trees, the *taiga,* or "land of little sticks." Despite the wind, or maybe because of it, the view was breathtaking. In the distance we could see Mount McKinley.

Another chance encounter, this time with a small band of Dall sheep. This group seemed leery of our presence at first, but soon resumed grazing. Still, not wanting to disturb them, we gave them a wide berth.

(Above) Sunset is often a time of contemplation. The day's ski over, the tent pitched, and the evening meal simmering, there is time to steal a few minutes to just sit and watch the colors. To the south the Alaska Range beckoned.

(Right, facing page) Despite their bulk and dopey appearance, moose are surprisingly graceful creatures, moving silently through the dark spruce. As they stepped into the sunny clearing, I could see that they were well over seven feet tall at the shoulder and probably weighed close to twelve hundred pounds. The moose paused briefly, as if posing for my camera, their breath visible like huge puffs of steam. They then continued on, their long, spindly legs stepping delicately down a steep ravine on their way to a frozen creek.

(Right) For all its lack of people and wide open spaces, Alaska is not necessarily a land of peace and quiet. Just when you think you've got away from all the noise of the city, a bunch of cackling, amorous ptarmigan keep you up all night. The watercourse near our camp seemed to be the local hangout, its knee-high brush offering plenty of food and cover for the gregarious little grouse.

Sometimes, even with the most meticulous preparation, things don't go as planned. Our original intention had been to kayak around Cape Newenham, but after several days of waiting for the Bering Sea to calm down enough to paddle on, we eventually gave up and opted for the torturous portage across several miles of tussock meadow.

Finally getting a chance at some kayaking, we encountered these murres and puffins as we approached Pinnacle Rock at the beginning of Security Cove. Safely tucked away from foxes and other predators in the nooks and crannies of the sheer cliffs were the seabirds' black and white downy chicks.

(Above) Foxes are stereotyped for being sly and crafty; they are also curious and even brazen. This one posed in front of a dramatic view of Cape Peirce headland, renowned as some of the best scenery in Alaska. The wind here never stops, and as a result the plant life grows low to the ground, lush only in scattered, well-protected places.

(Right, facing page) Unlike foxes, walruses are not interested in being viewed by humans. We had to sneak up the sand hill on our bellies, being careful not to make any jerky movements that the nearsighted beasts could detect. Hundreds of walruses lay on the beach, and more came throughout the day and evening to stake out what little bit of territory was left for their bloated, blubbery bodies. The din of the crowd's constant growling over territory was quite loud. Occasionally a warning bellow would be followed by a decided poke from a tusk. Some bulls had only pegs to poke with, perhaps having lost their tusks in a previous battle. More impressive than the noise, however, was the enormous stench emanating from the waste of such a concentration of two-ton animals.

CHAPTER 4

The Far North

This region is the "real" Alaska to many visitors, a vast primitive land that stretches between the Alaska Range on the south to the Arctic Ocean on the north, and from the Canadian border on the east to the Seward Peninsula on the west. Within this expansive zone are some of Alaska's finest national parks and preserves. Campsites are abundant. Wildlife, while never common, is diverse and easily observed. One researcher called this "a sparer version of the Serengeti." Days (weeks) will go by without seeing another soul.

KILLIK AND COLVILLE RIVERS/GATES OF THE ARCTIC NATIONAL PARK AND PRESERVE

Our river trip beginning in Gates of the Arctic National Park was unique: five miles on Easter Creek, ninety miles on the Killik, and seventy miles on the Colville River. Along the way we enjoyed the peaceful sights. All around for miles the wide open, gently rolling valley offered a continual gradation of prairie colors as the sun made its way across the sky. Far off in the distance storm clouds loomed. The feel of the paddle dipped in the clear, cool water, stroke after stroke, was relaxing. Our movable blind helped us observe an uncommon abundance of wildlife. At one point we came upon three bull caribou who had stopped to drink at a quiet backwater. Their enormous racks made us respect the strength of the beast that had to carry them.

The Arctic National Wildlife Refuge is the last place in North America—
perhaps the world—where a complete range of arctic and subarctic
ecosystems survive intact. The refuge is located in the northeast corner of
the state, bisected by the Brooks Range, where there are valleys and
ridges that have probably never been trod upon by humans.

With nine-thousand-foot Mount Chamberlin in the background, our midday view revealed Lake Peters below and its replenishing river. Standing in a place such as this, the mists of the high altitude all around your head, you can't help but imagine yourself a Greek god, high up on Olympus, ready to strike at some unsuspecting mortal.

Supreme Court Justice William O. Douglas enjoyed camping in Alaska. In 1960 while camped on the upper reaches of the Sheenjek River in the Brooks Range he wrote: "The Arctic has a call that is compelling. The distant mountains make one want to go on and on over the next ridge and over the one beyond. The call is that of a wilderness known only to a few. It is a call to adventure. This is not a place to possess like the plateaus of Wyoming or the valleys of Arizona; it is one to behold with wonderment. It is a domain for any restless soul who yearns to discover the startling beauties of creation in a place of quiet and solitude where life exists without molestation by man."

As we hiked through a valley in the Brooks Range we nearly collided with a wolverine. Wolverines are related to weasels and they are notoriously nasty. As soon as this one caught our scent, the thirty-pound animal reared up on his hind legs, peered at us over the hummocks, then began to bound toward us, growling a raspy growl all the way. He didn't seem to notice that we were six times his size. I stood up slowly and raised my hiking stick. "Get lost!" I shouted. That seemed to do it. He whirled around and disappeared into the high grass.

This lonely spur valley contained a fantastic combination of scenery. Early on, numerous little waterfalls delighted us with their gentle burbling sounds. Late in the day, however, walking through the narrow gorge gave one a feeling of being trapped; the walls were enormous eroded spires, parapets, and battlements, the floor a noisy gravel. We were loud and we were exposed. We encountered no animals but a few silly ptarmigan and wheatears. But the signs of Dall sheep—and grizzlies—were unmistakable.

We made camp on the orange tundra in the Sadlerochit Valley of the Brooks Range. The slopes of the mountains were only a few hundred feet above us, white with snow. The tundra's dull brown color and fading yellows and scarlets sadly indicated summer's end.

From the deep blues and reds of the alpine blueberry and cranberry, to the overwhelming splendor of the mountains and glaciers, to the grace and elegance of a bald eagle in flight—with so many vibrant colors, towering, powerful shapes, and delicate forms to take in, it is no wonder that I took hundreds of photographs. I hope you have enjoyed this small sampling.